MW01267736

GOING WILD

Climate and Nature

by Noah Leatherland

BEARPORT
PUBLISHING

Minneapolis, Minnesota

Credits
All images courtesy of Shutterstock. With thanks to Getty Images, Thinkstock Photo, and iStockphoto. Recurring images – Very_Very, Barbara.M.Mattson, Apostrophe, ArtKio, Ton Photographer 4289. Cover – Iyeyee, Oxima, Vectorpic. 2–3 – Peter Gudella. 4–5 – CSNafzger, Brent Coulter, Pung, Tonio_75. 6–7 – Ed Connor, Skreidzeleu, Nily.eps, waragon injan, Riccardo Mayer. 8–9 – Anton Balazh, Ion Mes, rigsbyphoto, Scott Book. 10–11 – ABO PHOTOGRAPHY, Olga Danylenko, small smiles, noomcpk, kamilpetran. 12–13 – BlueRingMedia, underworld, Tatiana Grozetskaya. 14–15 – MainlanderNZ, michelmond, justkgoomm, sun ok. 16–17 – Piyaset, smthtp, akramalrasny, amata90. 18–19 – yelantsevv, Bumble Dee, Volodymyr Burdiak, Stuedal, David Carbo. 20–21 – SARAWUT KUNDEJ, buttchi 3 Sha Life, Soo Jo, Stone36. 22–23 – Peter Gudella, chawalit khamsuk, AS photo family, Space-kraft, ShutterDesigner. 24–25 – Shaiith, Diyana Dimitrova, Zach Zimet, Evgeny_V. 26–27 – Creative Travel Projects, javarman, Kletr, Maridav. 28–29 – Ink Drop, f11photo, a katz, oneinchpunch, BongkarnGraphic. 30–31 – zhengzaishuru, Torychemistry.

Bearport Publishing Company Product Development Team
President: Jen Jenson; Director of Product Development: Spencer Brinker; Managing Editor: Allison Juda; Associate Editor: Naomi Reich; Associate Editor: Tiana Tran; Art Director: Colin O'Dea; Designer: Kim Jones; Designer: Kayla Eggert; Product Development Assistant: Owen Hamlin

Library of Congress Cataloging-in-Publication Data is available at www.loc.gov or upon request from the publisher.

ISBN: 979-8-88916-975-8 (hardcover)
ISBN: 979-8-89232-152-5 (ebook)

© 2025 BookLife Publishing
This edition is published by arrangement with BookLife Publishing.

For more information, write to Bearport Publishing, 5357 Penn Avenue South, Minneapolis, MN 55419.

CONTENTS

GOING WILD

The planet is made up of all kinds of different **biomes**: snowy mountains, hot deserts, thick forests, and flowering plains. Each biome has its own landscape and climate.

Different life can be found in each of these biomes, as each kind of landscape and climate makes certain kinds of **vegetation** grow. These plants clean the area's air and water, while also being a food source for some animals.

Plant-eating animals then become food for meat-eaters. When the plants and animals die, their remains break down to feed the soil for new vegetation to grow. This is how the life in an **ecosystem** is all connected.

A habitat is the place where a plant or animal lives.

Humans are also a part of ecosystems. Wherever we live, we share space with lots of plants and animals, but our actions can sometimes be harmful to them. Today, human activity is changing the climate worldwide, threatening the health of all living things.

WHAT IS CLIMATE?

A place's climate is the usual weather that happens there. This includes everything from how warm or cold it gets, how much rain or snow there is, or how windy it can be. Some places are cold and snow-covered all year. Others are warm and very rainy. Still other places have weather that changes with the seasons.

Many things determine a place's climate, such as whether it is near the **equator**, how far it is from the sea, and how high the land is.

The equator

People build their homes to be safe and comfortable within their particular climate. A climate can also affect the clothing a person wears. Farmers plant only those food crops that grow well in their climate.

A climate affects how people live their lives.

People are used to living with the expected weather their climate brings. So, a change to the climate has a big impact on people's daily lives.

CLIMATE CHANGE

Earth's climate has not always been what it is now. It has naturally changed over millions of years. Global temperatures have risen and fallen over time, sometimes getting hotter and sometimes getting colder.

Today, however, scientists have found that Earth's climate is changing faster than usual. This is because of things that humans are doing. Our actions are having a huge impact on the environment.

THE INDUSTRIAL REVOLUTION

In the 1800s, humans discovered new ways to power machines and factories by burning fossil fuels. These new methods used to create **energy** started the Industrial Revolution.

Fossil fuels are made from plants and animals that died millions of years ago.

Scientists have since discovered that Earth's climate has been changing dramatically since fossil fuels began powering our world.

CARBON STORES

Carbon is an **element** that is essential to life on Earth. Carbon exists in the ground, the **atmosphere**, and the oceans. It is also the main element in the bodies of plants and animals. The places where carbon is found are called carbon stores.

In the atmosphere, carbon exists as a gas called carbon dioxide. This gas acts like a heavy blanket, trapping Earth's heat and making it warm enough to support life. But too much carbon dioxide in the atmosphere can be harmful.

Trees pull lots of carbon dioxide out of the air to make their food. For a long time, this kept the gas from building up in the atmosphere.

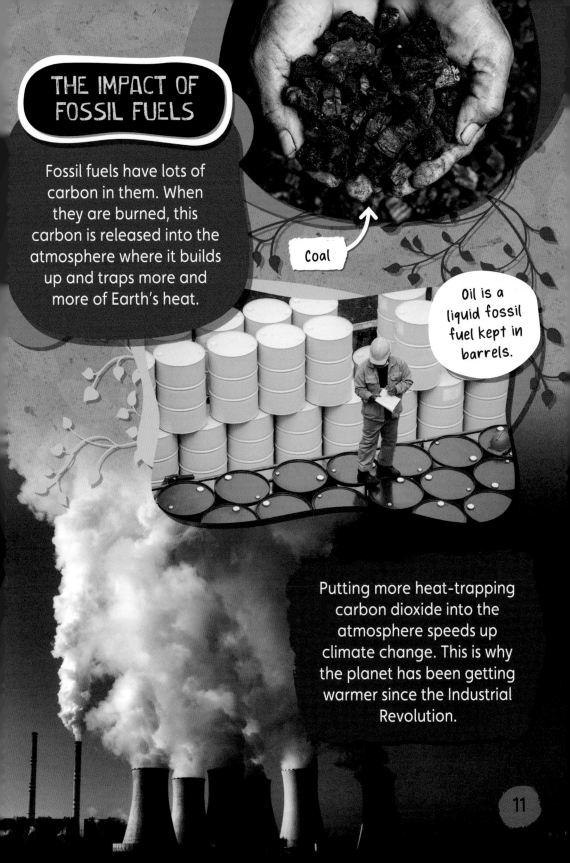

THE IMPACT OF FOSSIL FUELS

Fossil fuels have lots of carbon in them. When they are burned, this carbon is released into the atmosphere where it builds up and traps more and more of Earth's heat.

Coal

Oil is a liquid fossil fuel kept in barrels.

Putting more heat-trapping carbon dioxide into the atmosphere speeds up climate change. This is why the planet has been getting warmer since the Industrial Revolution.

THE GREENHOUSE EFFECT

Carbon dioxide is a kind of greenhouse gas. When the sun heats Earth, some of the heat gets trapped by these greenhouse gases and keeps the planet warm. This is known as the greenhouse effect.

Greenhouse gases trap much of the sun's heat in the atmosphere.

Some heat bounces back into space.

By using fossil fuels to power our cars, homes, businesses, and factories, we are pumping a lot more carbon dioxide into the atmosphere. This means more of the sun's heat is being trapped, making the planet warmer. The rise in Earth's temperatures is called global warming.

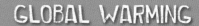

GLOBAL WARMING

Rising global temperatures are changing normal weather patterns. Some ecosystems are getting a lot hotter and drier. The plants and animals in these changing areas often struggle to survive the new conditions.

Some parts of the world aren't getting hotter. However, that does not mean climate change isn't affecting them. Climate change impacts weather in all sorts of ways. So, even places that are getting colder are experiencing climate change.

CLIMATE CHANGE AND HUMANS

RISING SEA LEVELS

The rising temperatures that come with global warming are causing large ice sheets and glaciers in Antarctica and the Arctic to melt. The water enters the oceans, causing sea levels to rise.

Rising sea levels means floods are more likely along coastlines, often forcing people out of their homes. Experts say that some coastal cities and towns may be completely underwater within 50 years.

EXTREME WEATHER

A changing climate causes shifts in normal global wind patterns, sending weather to unexpected places. In some parts of the world, summers are much hotter with more long heat waves. In other places, winters are becoming much colder.

Warmer ocean waters **evaporate** more moisture into the atmosphere. The increased heat rising off the ocean also creates stronger winds. When stronger winds combine with this extra moisture, the result is more frequent and destructive superstorms, including hurricanes.

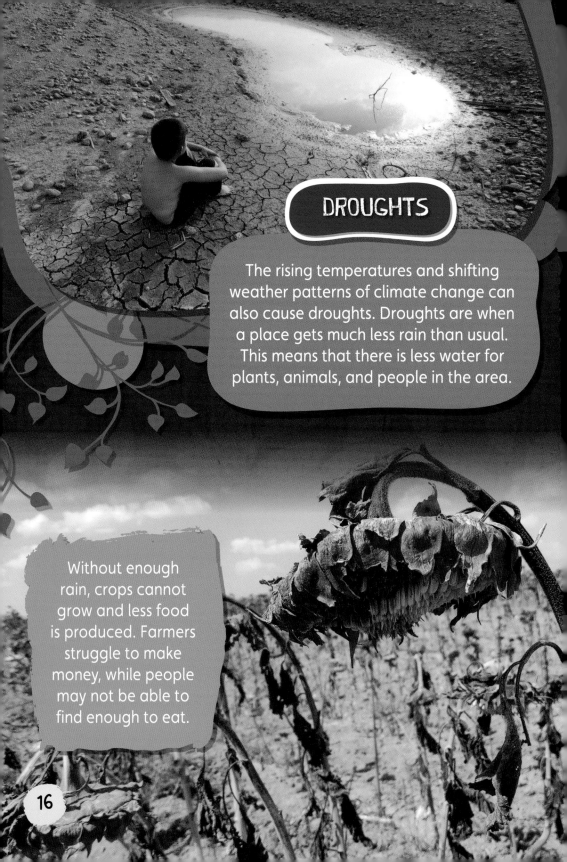

DROUGHTS

The rising temperatures and shifting weather patterns of climate change can also cause droughts. Droughts are when a place gets much less rain than usual. This means that there is less water for plants, animals, and people in the area.

Without enough rain, crops cannot grow and less food is produced. Farmers struggle to make money, while people may not be able to find enough to eat.

DISPLACEMENT

When people are forced to move away from their homes, it is called displacement. Climate change can make some places too tough to live in. Droughts, rising sea levels, monster storms, and flooding force people from their homes.

These displaced people are sometimes called climate refugees.

The displaced people need to find somewhere else to live, sometimes overcrowding nearby areas. This can put even more stress on the environment.

CLIMATE CHANGE AND ANIMALS

WILDFIRES

Warmer temperatures and less rainfall can make forests very dry, sparking wildfires that are very hard to put out. They can burn down large parts of forests.

Wildfires can kill woodland animals or destroy their habitats, leaving them without homes. Wildfires also destroy plants, taking away food and shelter that animals need for survival.

MELTING ICE

Lots of animals live on and around the ice in the Arctic and Antarctica. As the ice melts, it becomes harder for these animals to find food and make their homes.

Melting ice causes sea levels to rise. Coastal habitats can be flooded or destroyed when salt water moves in and covers the land. Many plants cannot survive in salt water, and the coastal creatures who rely on them for food and shelter must move or die.

Rising sea levels make it harder for turtles to find dry beaches to lay their eggs.

CORAL BLEACHING

Not only are the oceans rising, but they are also getting warmer.

A healthy coral reef

When coral loses its algae, it goes white.

Coral reefs provide food and shelter to thousands of sea creatures and plants. They also store lots of carbon that would otherwise enter the atmosphere. Coral reefs are covered in **algae**, which feed them and give them color. Warmer oceans make the reefs shed algae, lose their color, and die.

SEASONAL CHANGES

Many animals use the changing of the seasons to know when to migrate, have their young, or hibernate.

Changing climates affect how seasons change. This can throw off the timing of when animals look for nesting areas, have babies, or search for food and shelter.

A change to the seasons also causes some plants to **bloom** at unusual times. If these plants produce fruit earlier than usual, the animals that typically rely on them for food may miss out later.

RENEWABLE ENERGY

The burning of fossil fuels adds a lot of carbon dioxide into the atmosphere. This makes the greenhouse effect stronger, heating the planet and speeding up climate change.

To help slow climate change, scientists have found ways of making energy without burning fossil fuels. Renewable energy comes from natural resources that will not run out. By using renewable energy instead of fossil fuels, less carbon is put into the atmosphere and climate change is slowed.

WIND ENERGY

Wind turbines are tall towers with long blades. As the wind hits these blades, it pushes them around. This rotation makes electricity that can be used for power. The turbines are usually placed in areas that get a lot of strong wind, such as in the water near the shore or on hills and mountains.

A wind turbine

A group of turbines is called a wind farm.

23

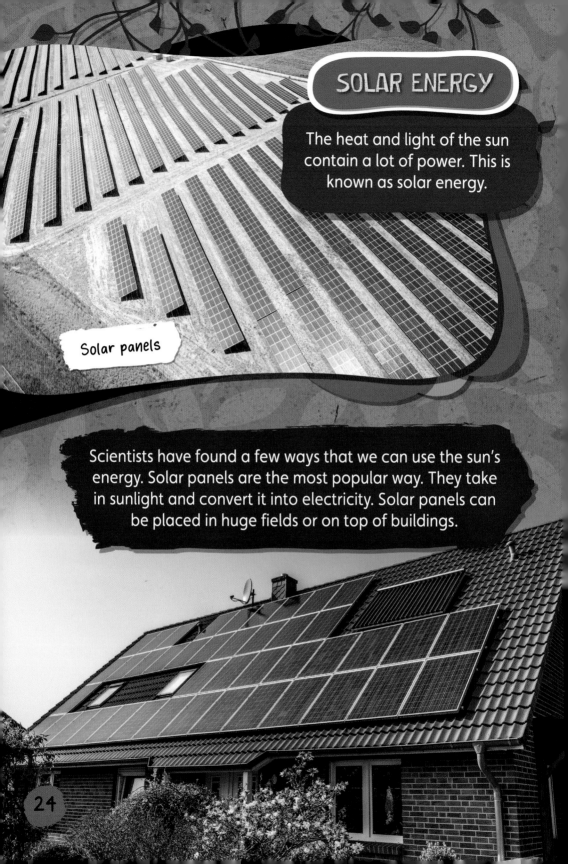

SOLAR ENERGY

The heat and light of the sun contain a lot of power. This is known as solar energy.

Solar panels

Scientists have found a few ways that we can use the sun's energy. Solar panels are the most popular way. They take in sunlight and convert it into electricity. Solar panels can be placed in huge fields or on top of buildings.

HYDROELECTRIC ENERGY

People have used the power of water for a long time. Hundreds of years ago, rivers were used to turn wheels that ground wheat into flour. Now, hydroelectric power uses water to make electricity.

Water wheels are some of the oldest ways that people have used nature to make power.

One way flowing water can be used to make electricity is by turning turbines, just as wind turbines make power. Hydroelectric dams are built into rivers. They use the power of flowing water to turn huge turbines.

A hydroelectric dam

GEOTHERMAL ENERGY

More than 1,800 miles (3,000 km) below the ground is Earth's extremely hot core. Temperatures there can get hotter than 9,000 degrees Fahrenheit (5,000 degrees Celsius). The core's heat warms underground rocks, water, and gas.

Steam created by the core's heat can be used to spin turbines and make electricity. This is called geothermal energy.

A geothermal power plant

BIOMASS ENERGY

This power plant uses renewable biomass to generate electricity.

Biomass is material that came from living things, such as dead plants, animal waste, and rotting food. Biomass can be used to create fuel and to generate energy. The heat created by burning wood in a fireplace is a form of biomass energy.

Biofuel can be created by breaking down biomass. This can then be used instead of fossil fuels to power some cars.

RAISING YOUR VOICE

While ordinary people can do their part to cut back on using fossil fuel, the biggest users are large companies. They burn the most fuel and put the most heat-trapping carbon dioxide into the atmosphere. Still, ordinary people can use their voices to speak up for change.

BOYCOTTS

When companies cause harm to the environment, people can boycott them. This means choosing not to buy any more of their goods. If enough people boycott, companies may be forced to change.

Some people boycott companies with products that use palm oil because palm oil plantations can damage the environment.

PROTESTS

A protest is when a group of people gathers to demand change. Protests usually happen in big public spaces to be seen by lots of people. Protestors might make signs or yell chants about their cause.

WRITING LETTERS

Politicians are elected to help the people in their area. If you are concerned about the environment, write to your representatives and let them know. Ask them what they are doing to help or give them your own ideas!

29

A BETTER FUTURE

Climate change is a big problem, but there are lots of people hard at work to help. They are finding ways to reduce the use of fossil fuels and adopt renewable energy sources. Together, we can slow down climate change.

The best way to tackle climate change is by doing it together. People can use their voices to make change happen. If we all work together, we can be sure there is a better future for our planet.

GLOSSARY

algae plantlike living things often found in water

atmosphere the mixture of gases that make up the air surrounding Earth

biomes regions with a particular climate and environment where certain kinds of plants and animals live

bloom to flower or blossom

carbon a natural element found in coal, oil, and in the bodies of living things

ecosystem a community of living things and the environment they live in

element a pure substance made from only one type of atom

energy a type of power, such as light or heat, that can be used to do something

equator the imaginary line around Earth that is an equal distance from the north and south poles

evaporate to turn liquid water into water vapor

politicians people who work in the government

vegetation plant life

INDEX

READ MORE

Gehl, Laura. *Climate Warriors: Fourteen Scientists and Fourteen Ways We Can Save Our Planet.* Minneapolis: Millbrook Press, 2023.

Henzel, Cynthia Kennedy. *Redesigning Cities to Fight Climate Change (Fighting Climate Change with Science).* Lake Elmo, MN: Focus Readers, 2023.

Starr, Abbe L. *Climate Change Solutions (Searchlight Books—Spotlight on Climate Change).* Minneapolis: Lerner Publications, 2023.

LEARN MORE ONLINE

1. Go to **www.factsurfer.com** or scan the QR code below.

2. Enter "**Wild Climate**" into the search box.

3. Click on the cover of this book to see a list of websites.